Solving Science Questions

A Book About the Scientific Process

Rachel M. Chappell

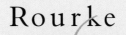

Rourke
Publishing LLC
Vero Beach, Florida 32964

www.rourkepublishing.com

PHOTO CREDITS: title page © Sebastian Kaulitzki; page 4 © Elaine Davis; page 5 © Paulaphoto; page 6 © Vadim Koziovsky; page 7 © Patrick Hermans; page 8 © Philip Date; page 9 © Sebastian Kaulitzki; page 10 © Kanwarjit Singh Boparai; page 11 © Sonja Foos; page 12 © Sebastian Kaulitzki; page 14 © Galina Barskaya; page 15 © Patrick Hermans; page 16 © Costing Cojocavu; page 20 © Leah-Anne Thompson; page 22 © Hashim Pudiyapura.

Editor: Robert Stengard-Olliges

Cover design by Michelle Moore.

Library of Congress Cataloging-in-Publication Data

Chappell, Rachel M., 1978-
  Solving science questions : a book about the scientific process / Rachel M. Chappell.
    p. cm. -- (Big ideas for young scientists)
  Includes index. 41038018 6/09
  ISBN 978-1-60044-542-2 (Hardcover)
  ISBN 978-1-60044-703-7 (Softcover)
  1. Science--Methodology--Juvenile literature. 2. Research--Methodology--Juvenile literature. I. Title.
  Q175.C459 2008
  501--dc22
                        2007018237

Printed in the USA

CG/CG

Rourke Publishing

www.rourkepublishing.com – rourke@rourkepublishing.com
Post Office Box 3328, Vero Beach, FL 32964

Table of Contents

Asking Questions and Researching

Hmm…do you ever wonder? Scientists wonder, or have questions about lots of things. When scientists have questions they want to answer, they go through a process to find a solution.

Scientists start with a **question**. Then they **research** information about their question, or problem.

Jayme thinks like a scientist and asks many questions. Today she's wondering, "What brand of bubble bath makes the most bubbles?" Jayme uses books and the internet to look for information about bubbles. She learns how bubbles form and the different solutions used to make them.

Forming a Hypothesis

Next, scientists make a thoughtful guess, or **hypothesis**. The hypothesis is what scientists think the answer might be to the question they are asking.

Jayme chooses three brands of bubble bath to compare. She makes the hypothesis that the most expensive brand of bubble bath will make the most bubbles.

Gathering Materials

Gathering materials and performing the **experiment** are the next two steps in the process. Scientists gather their materials, set up the experiment, and then do the experiment to test their hypothesis.

Materials Jayme Needs

- *Three clear 1 liter containers labeled A, B, C*
- *Three different kinds of bubble bath labeled A, B, C*
- *Water*
- *Straws*
- *Timer*
- *Ruler*

Trials and Variables

During experiments, scientists always perform tests several times. They call these tests **trials**. In each trial, scientists change only one thing.

Jayme puts the same amount of water and bubble bath in each container for each test. The only change, or **variable**, is the brand of bubble bath she uses.

Experimenting

Scientists keep **journals** as they research and experiment. They record important information, numbers, charts, graphs, **observations**, and **results**.

Steps for Testing Bubble Bath

1. Pour 100 ml of water into the container labeled A. Pour 10 ml of bubble bath A into the same container.
2. Put the straw into the mixture and blow for 5 seconds.
3. Measure the height of the bubbles using a ruler. Start from the water line.
4. Repeat steps one through three for bubble baths B and C.
5. Repeat the trial two more times.
6. Record the results each time on the chart.

Next, Jayme follows the steps and performs the experiment.

Put straw in container

Blow for 5 seconds

Measure bubbles starting from the water line

Repeat on other containers

Results and Conclusion

Results for Bubble Bath Experiment

Bubble Bath	Trial 1	Trail 2	Trail 3
A Least Expensive			
B Most Expen			

After each test, scientists record their results. They use **charts** and graphs to show what they learned during the experiments.

Results for Bubble Bath Experiment

Bubble Bath	Trial 1	Trial 2	Trial 3
A (Least expensive)	6 cm	9 cm	8 cm
B (Most expensive)	5 cm	6 cm	5 cm
C	6 cm	3 cm	4 cm

Jayme uses the computer to create a chart for reporting her bubble bath results.

Forming **conclusions** is the next step in the process. A scientist's conclusion is what the scientist learned from the results of the experiment.

Jayme's hypothesis is incorrect. In most of the trials, bubble bath A, the lowest-priced brand, made the greatest amount of bubbles. What a surprise!

Sharing Discoveries with the World

Scientists write reports and give talks so everyone can benefit from what they learned by asking questions, researching, and experimenting.

Jayme shares what she discovered, too. Now all her classmates know which bubble bath to buy if they like bunches of bubbles!

Glossary

conclusion (kuhn KLOO zhuhn) – the inference or deduction made after the results of an experiment are complete

experiments (ek SPER uh muhnts) – tests or trials done with the purpose to discover something new or to prove something

hypothesis (hahy POTH uh sis) – a reasonable guess

observation (ob zur VAY shuhn) – the act of noting and recording something

question (KWESS chuhn) – a problem for discussion, a matter of investigation

research (REE surch) – investigating a subject in order to discover or revise facts

results (ri ZYHLTS) – the outcome or effects of an experiment

trials (TRYE uhlz) – a group of tests in an experiment

variable (VAIR ee uh buhl) – something that changes

Index

Further Reading

Ardley, Neil. *101 Great Science Experiments*. DK
  Publishing, 2006.
Freeman, Marcia S. and Sheehan, Thomas F. *You are a
  Scientist*. Rourke Classroom Resources, 2004.
Whitley, Peggy. *99 Jumpstarts for Kid's Science Research*.
  Libraries Unlimited, 2006.

Websites to Visit

homeschooling.gomilpitas.com/explore
www.biology4kids.com
www.uga.edu/srel/kidsdoscience/kidsdoscience.htm

About the Author

Rachel M. Chappell graduated from the University of South
Florida. She enjoys teaching boys and girls as well as their
teachers. She lives in Sarasota, Florida and gets excited
about reading and writing in her spare time. Her family
consists of a husband, one son, and a dog named Sadie.